PIGS
Trace Taylor

This is a pig.

This is a pig.

This pig lives on a farm.

This pig lives in the woods.

This pig can go here.

This pig can go here.

The pig on the farm will get food.

The pig in the woods has to look for food.

The pig on a farm gets farm food.

The pig in the woods gets what it can.

Animals can't get the farm pig.

Animals can get the wood pig.

This is a baby farm pig.

This is a baby wood pig.

15

A farm pig has baby pigs.

A wood pig has baby pigs.

 The baby farm pig will live on the farm.

The baby wood pig will live in the woods.

I can use the first letter sound to match the word to the picture

pig

woods

baby

farm